SOMETHING *new* FOR THE GIRLS

Arranged by DAN COATES

for easy piano

W9-ACC-595

CONTENTS

YOU RAISE ME UP

Words and Music by
ROLF LOVLAND and BRENDAN GRAHAM
Arranged by DAN COATES

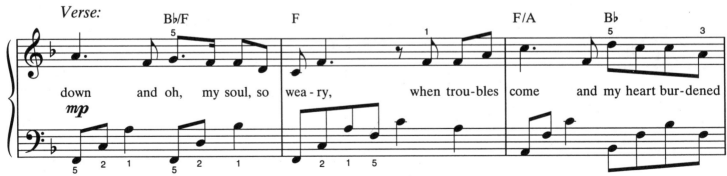

You Raise Me Up - 4 - 1

Chorus:

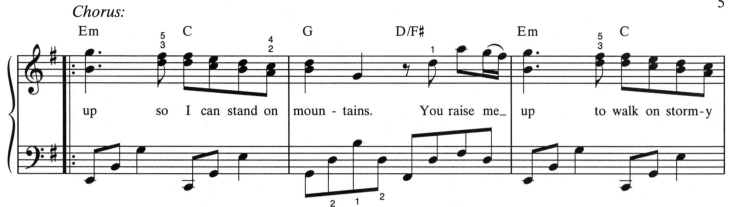

up so I can stand on moun - tains. You raise me_ up to walk on storm-y

seas. I am strong when I am on your shoul - ders. You raise me

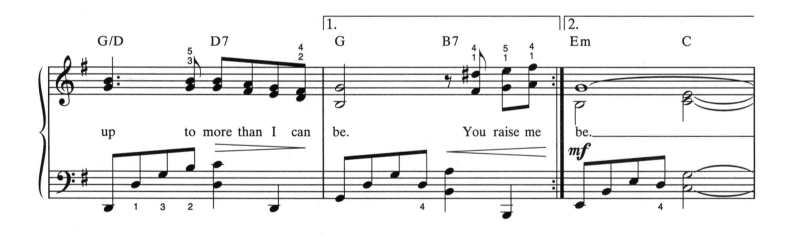

up to more than I can be. You raise me be._

You raise me up to more than_ I can be.

BREAKAWAY

Words and Music by
MATTHEW GERRARD, AVRIL LAVIGNE
and BRIDGET BENENATE
Arranged by DAN COATES

Da da da___ da da, da da da___ da da, da da da___

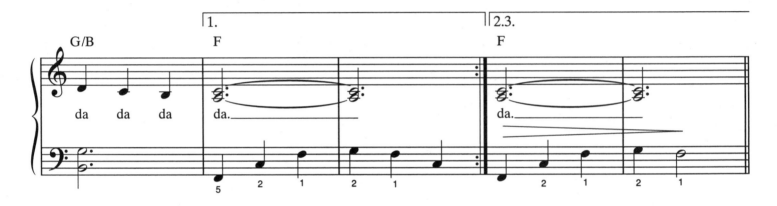

da da da da.___ da.___

Verse:

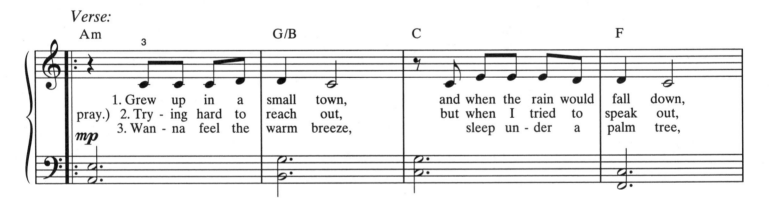

1. Grew up in a small town, and when the rain would fall down,
(pray.) 2. Try-ing hard to reach out, but when I tried to speak out,
3. Wan-na feel the warm breeze, sleep un-der a palm tree,

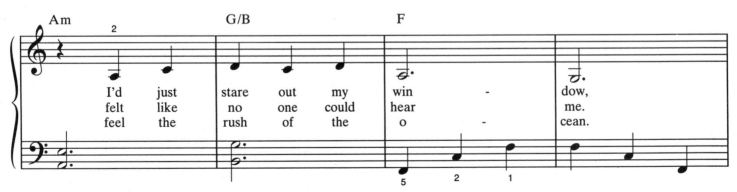

I'd just stare out my win - dow,
felt like no one could hear me.
feel the rush of the o - cean.

DANCE WITH MY FATHER

Words and Music by
LUTHER VANDROSS
and RICHARD MARX
Arranged by DAN COATES

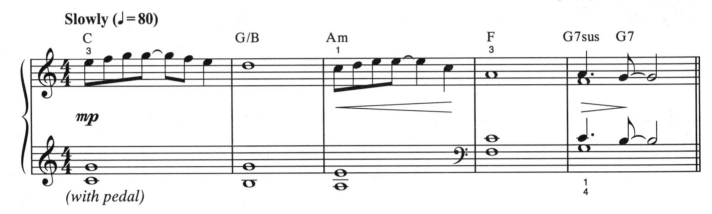

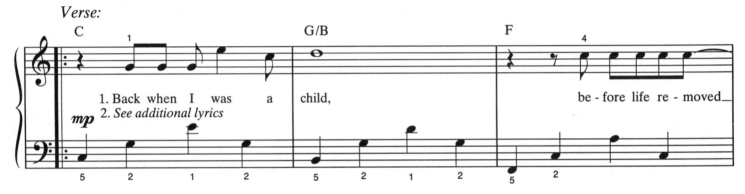

Dance With My Father - 4 - 1

12

Verse 2:
When I and my mother would disagree,
To get my way, I would run from her to him.
He'd make me laugh just to comfort me,
Then finally make me do just what my mama said.
Later that night, when I was asleep,
He'd left a dollar under my sheet.
Never dreamed that would be gone from me.

Chorus 2:
If I could steal one final glance,
One final step,
One final dance with him,
I'd play a song that would never, ever end.
'Cause I'd love, love, love
To dance with my father again.

BELIEVER

Words and Music by
will.i.am and John Legend
Arranged by DAN COATES

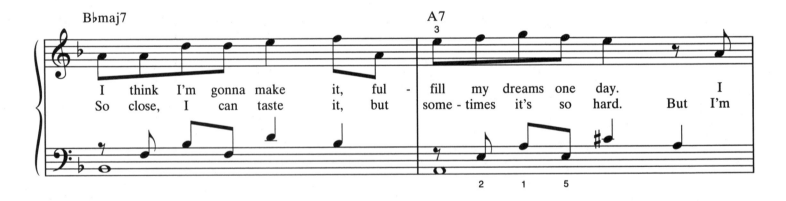

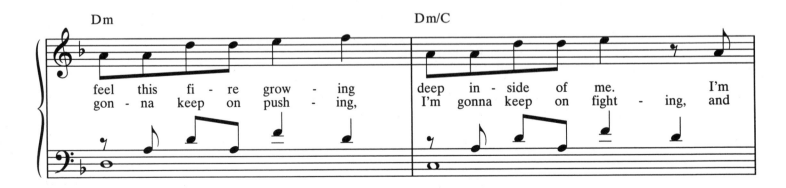

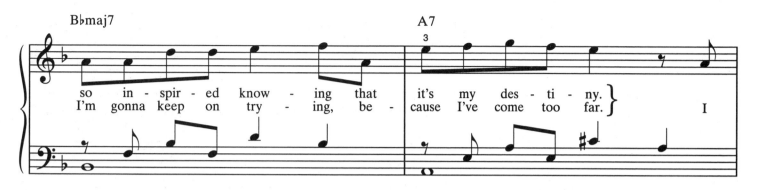

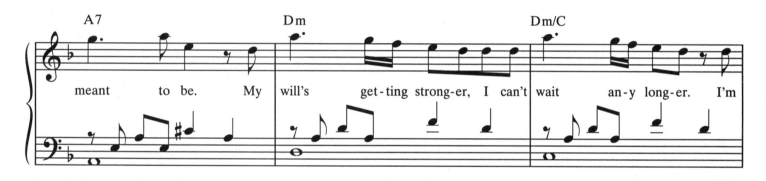

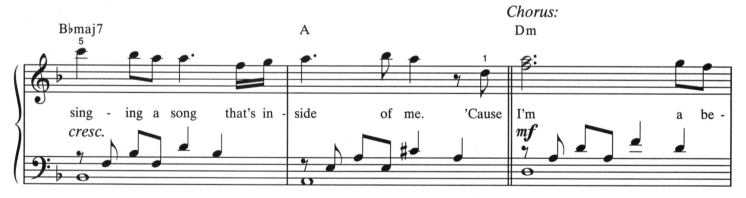

DON'T CRY OUT LOUD

Words and Music by
PETER ALLEN and CAROLE BAYER SAGER
Arranged by DAN COATES

Slowly, with expression

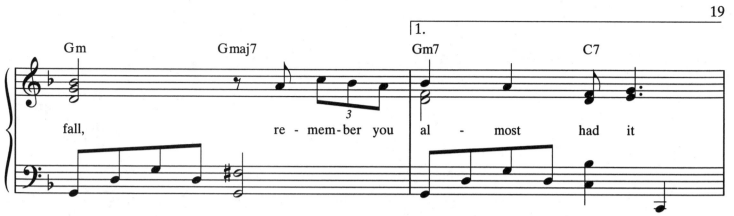

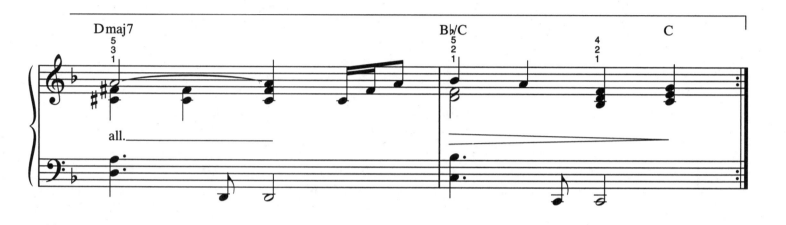

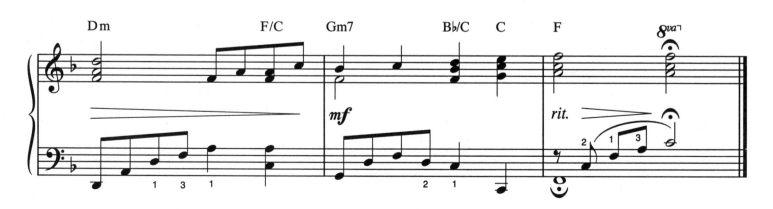

8TH WORLD WONDER

Words and Music by
KYLE JACOBS, SHAUN SHANKEL
and JOEL PARKES
Arranged by DAN COATES

With a moderate, steady beat (♩ = 100)

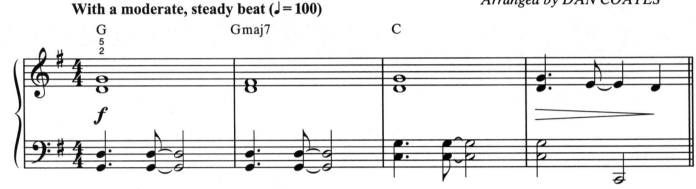

Verse:

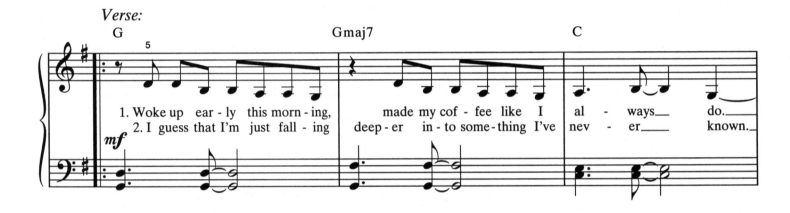

1. Woke up ear-ly this morn-ing, made my cof-fee like I al-ways___ do.
2. I guess that I'm just fall-ing deep-er in-to some-thing I've nev-er___ known.

Then it hit me from no-where, ev-'ry-thing I feel a-bout
But the way that I'm feel-ing makes me re-al-ize that it

me and___ you.
can't be___ wrong.

The way___ you
Your love's like a

kiss me cra - zy.
sum - mer rain,_____

Ba - by,___ you're
wash - ing___ my

so a - maz - ing.
doubts a - way._____

cresc.

Chorus:

Sev - en days and sev - en nights of thun - der.

The wa - ter's ris - ing and I'm___

f

___ slip - ping un - der.

I think I fell in love___ with the eighth___ world won-

1.

der._____

Yeah, yeah, yeah._____

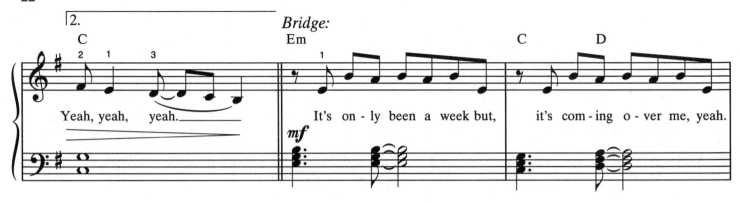

Yeah, yeah, yeah. It's on-ly been a week but, it's com-ing o-ver me, yeah.

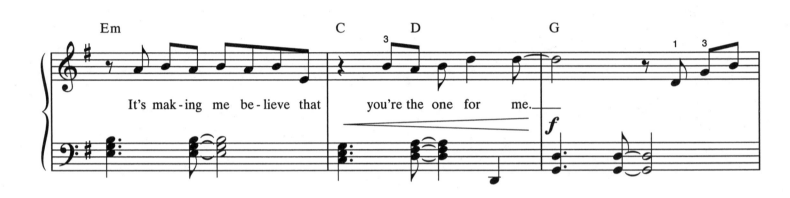

It's mak-ing me be-lieve that you're the one for me.

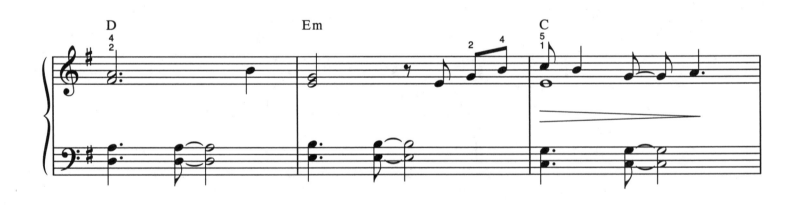

FLY

Words and Music by
JOHN SHANKS and KARA DIOGUARDI
Arranged by DAN COATES

Moderately slow

Verses 1 & 2:

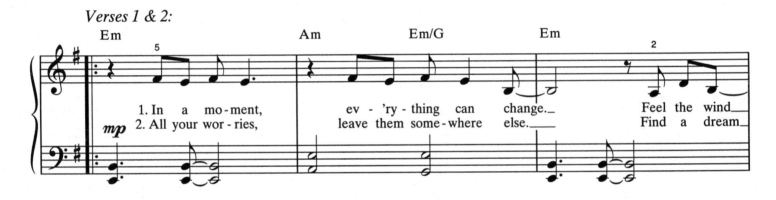

1. In a mo-ment, ev-'ry-thing can change.___ Feel the wind___
2. All your wor-ries, leave them some-where else.___ Find a dream___

___ on your shoul-der. For a min-ute, all the world can wait.___
___ you can fol-low. Reach for some-thing when there's noth-ing left___

Let go___ of your yes-ter-day. Can you hear it call-ing?
and the world's feel-ing hol-low.___

Fly - 4 - 1

LIGHT IN YOUR EYES

Words and Music by
SHERYL CROW and JOHN SHANKS
Arranged by DAN COATES

Moderately, with a steady beat (♩ = 108)

Verses 1 & 2:

1. Some-thing is hap - p'ning,_____ ev - 'ry-thing's dif -
2. No use pre - tend - ing._____ You nev - er ex - ist -

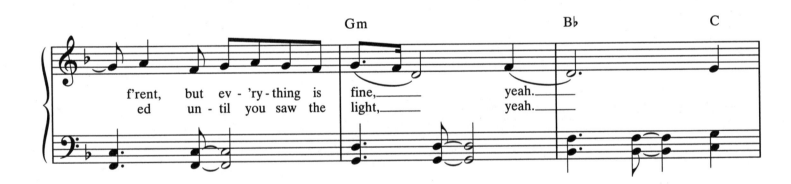

f'rent, but ev - 'ry-thing is fine,_____ yeah._____
ed un - til you saw the light,_____ yeah._____

This is the good___ stuff,_____ yes - ter-day's on -
You're just be - gin - ning._____ You have - n't missed_

Light in Your Eyes - 4 - 1

Chorus:

THE NOTEBOOK
(Main Title)

Written by
AARON ZIGMAN
Arranged by DAN COATES

Slowly, with expression (♩ = 69)

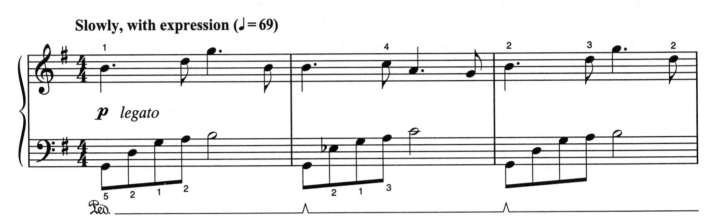

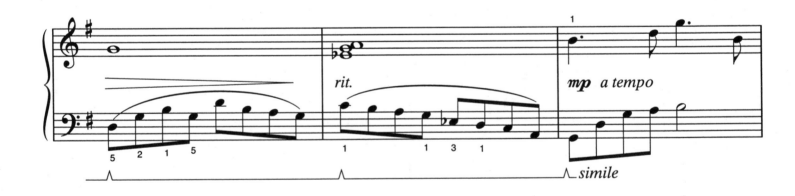

The Notebook - 3 - 1

34

THE REASON

Words and Music by
DANIEL ESTRIN and DOUGLAS ROBB
Arranged by DAN COATES

Moderately slow

Verse:

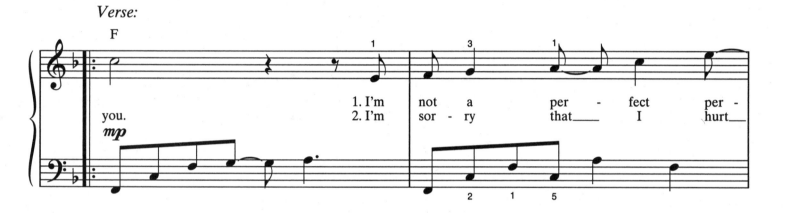

1. I'm not a per - fect per - son
2. I'm sor - ry that I hurt you,

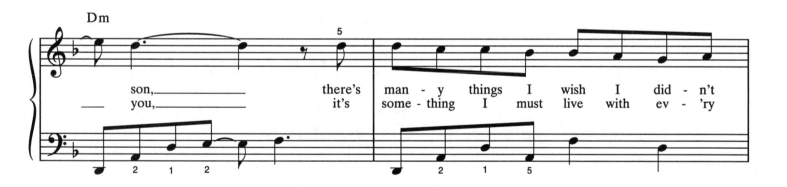

there's man - y things I wish I did - n't do.
it's some - thing I must live with ev - 'ry day.

But I con - tin - ue learn - ing
And all the pain I put you
3. I'm not a per - fect per -

Chorus:

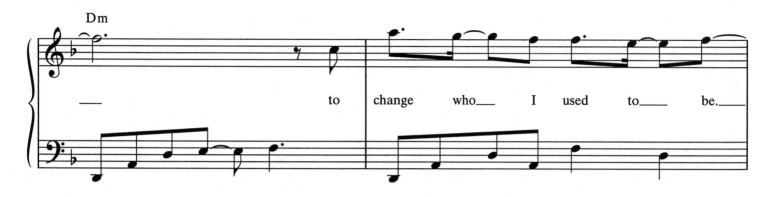

to change who___ I used to___ be.___

To Coda ⊕

___ A rea - son___ to start o - ver

1.

new, and the rea - son___ is

2.

new, and the rea - son___ is

Bridge:

you,

and the rea - son___ is

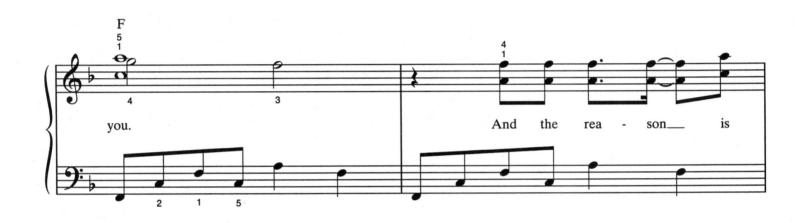

you.

And the rea - son___ is

you,

and the rea - son is___

D.S. 𝄋 al Coda

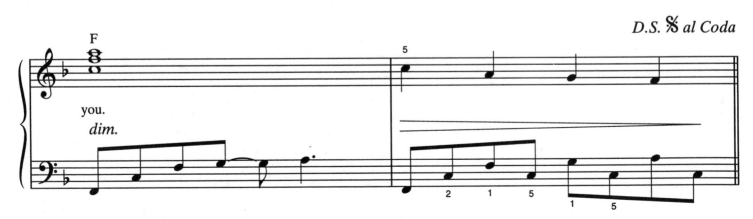

you.

dim.

OLDER THAN MY YEARS

Words and Music by
PAUL MOESSL and KEVIN HUGHES
Arranged by DAN COATES

Slowly, with expression

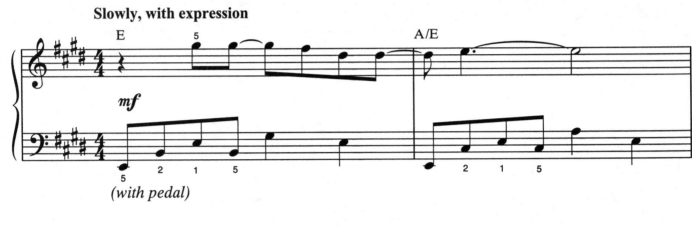

(with pedal)

Verse:

1. You say___ that you are leav-ing,___ they say___ that I'm too
2. You say___ that life's a jour-ney,___ they say___ I'm on-ly

young for you. You say___ it's for the bet-ter, and that
at the start. You say___ it's a be-gin-ning, but it

Older Than My Years - 4 - 1

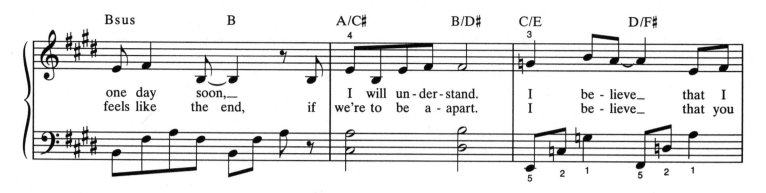

Chorus:

TAKE MY BREATH AWAY

By
GIORGIO MORODER and TOM WHITLOCK
Arranged by DAN COATES

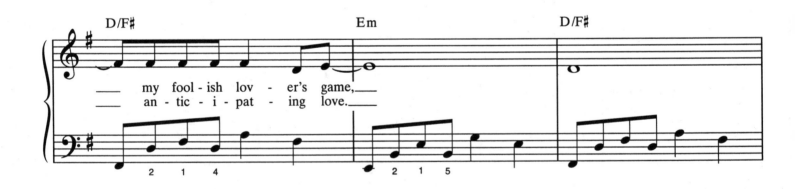

Take My Breath Away - 4 - 1

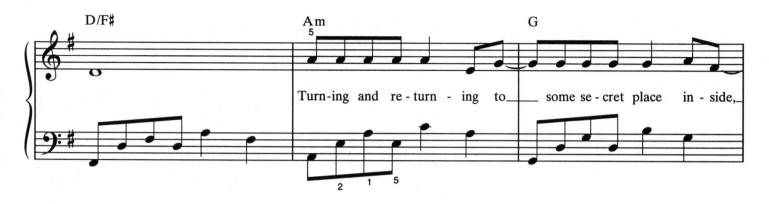

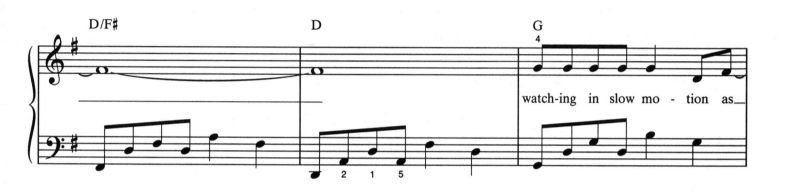

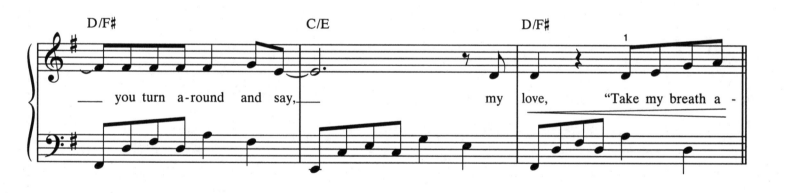

Chorus:

Take my breath a - | way."

dim.

Bridge:

Through the ho - ur glass I saw___ you. In time, you slipped___ a - way.

mf

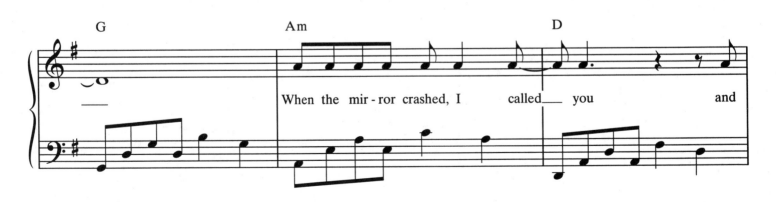

___ When the mir - ror crashed, I called___ you and

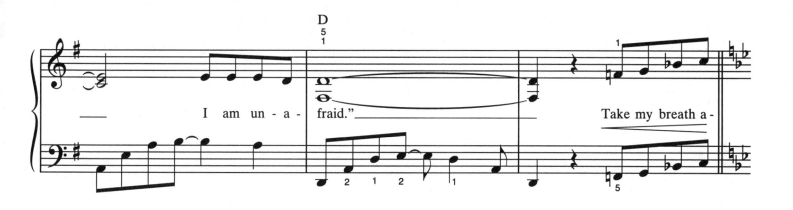

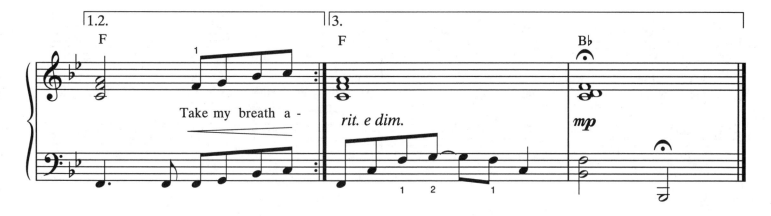

From Touchstone Pictures' "PEARL HARBOR"

THERE YOU'LL BE

Words and Music by
DIANE WARREN
Arranged by DAN COATES

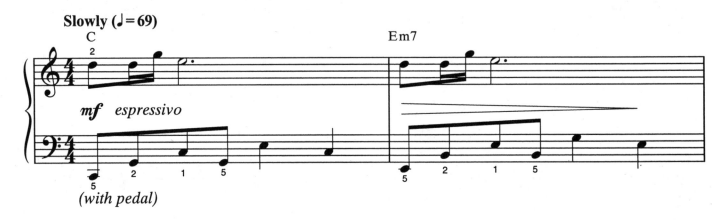

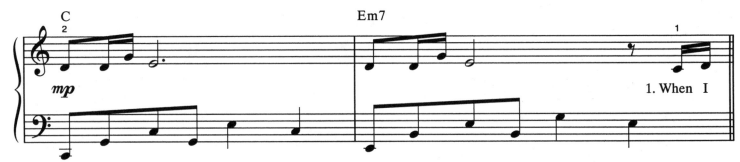

Verse:

think back on these times and the dreams we left be-hind, I'll be
showed me how it feels to feel the sky with-in my reach. And I

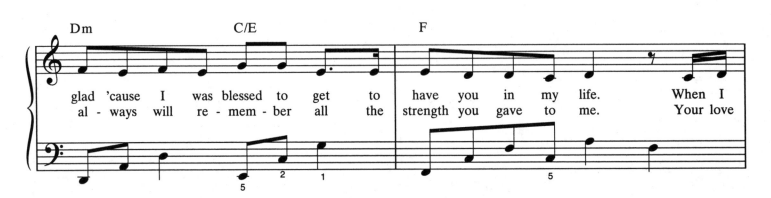

glad 'cause I was blessed to get to have you in my life. When I
al-ways will re-mem-ber all the strength you gave to me. Your love

There You'll Be - 5 - 1

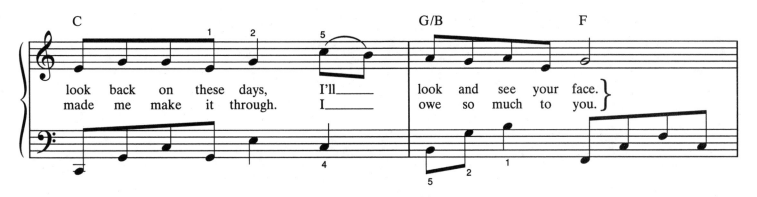

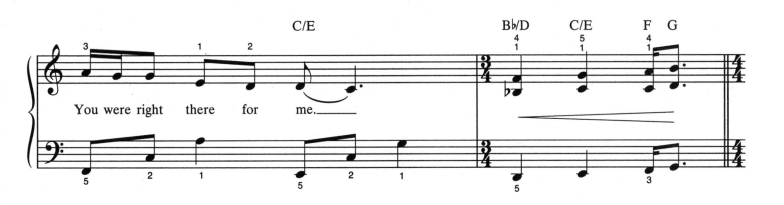

Chorus:

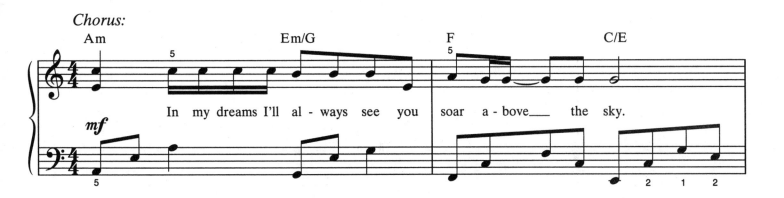

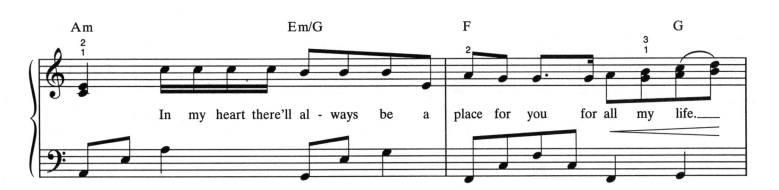

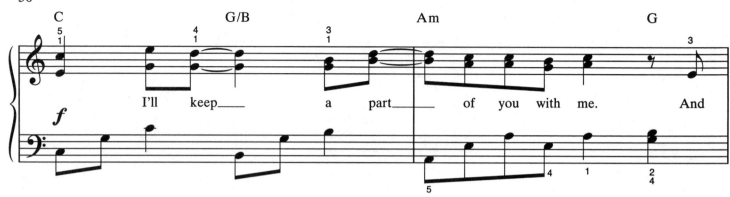

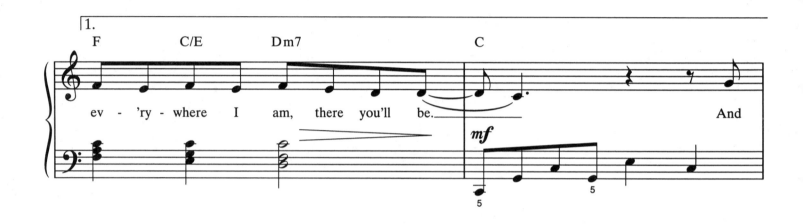

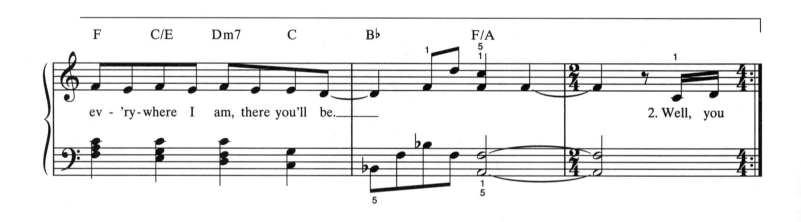

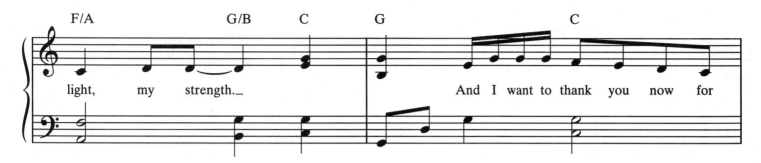

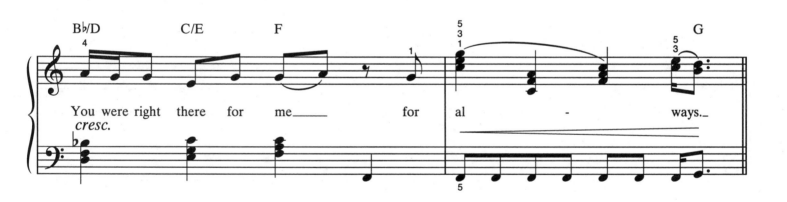

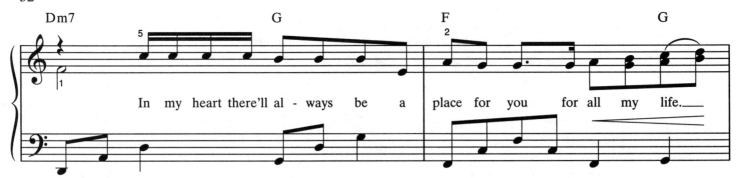

In my heart there'll al - ways be a place for you for all my life.

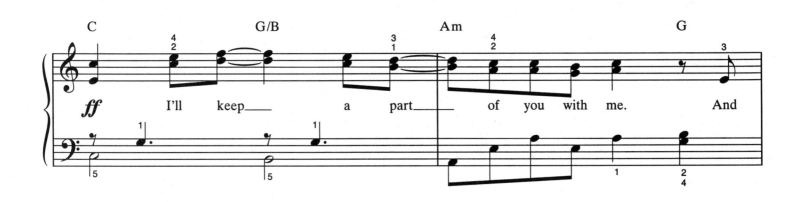

I'll keep a part of you with me. And

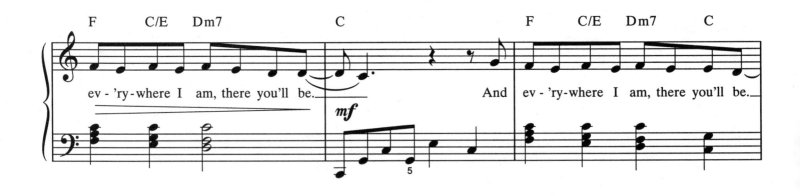

ev - 'ry-where I am, there you'll be. And ev - 'ry-where I am, there you'll be.

There you'll be.

rit. e dim.

THIS IS THE NIGHT

Words and Music by
CHRISTOPHER BRAIDE, GARY BURR
and ALDO NOVA
Arranged by DAN COATES

Majestically (♩ = 50)

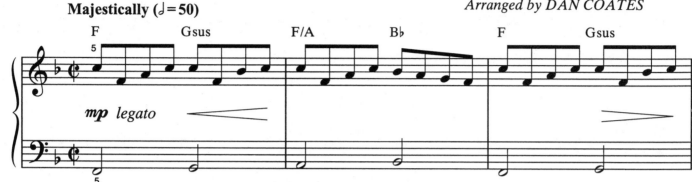

1. When the world was-n't up-side down,___ I could

take all the time___ I had.___ But I'm not gon-na wait___ when a mo-

ment can van-ish so fast.___ 'Cause

This Is the Night - 5 - 1

TO WHERE YOU ARE

Words and Music by
RICHARD MARX and
LINDA THOMPSON
Arranged by DAN COATES

To Where You Are - 5 - 1

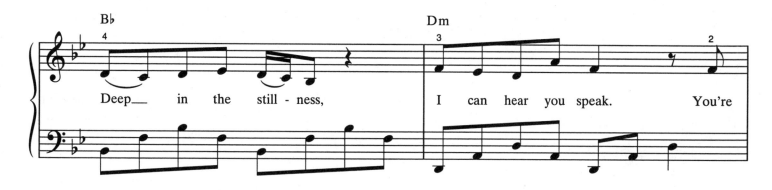

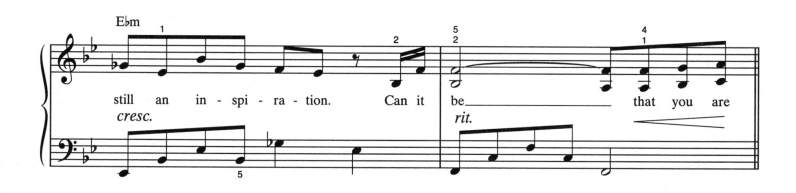

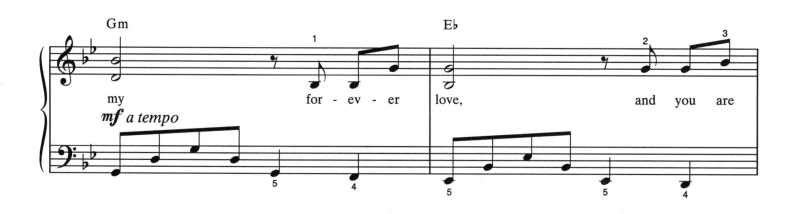

THE WAY

Words and Music by
DAVID SIEGEL, STEVE MORALES,
KARA DIOGUARDI and ENRIQUE IGLESIAS
Arranged by DAN COATES

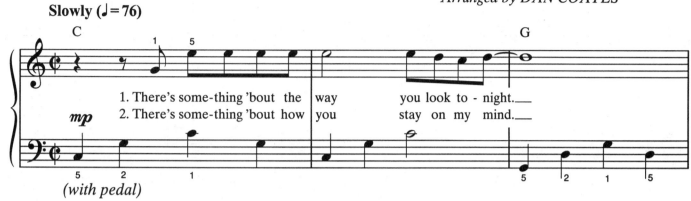

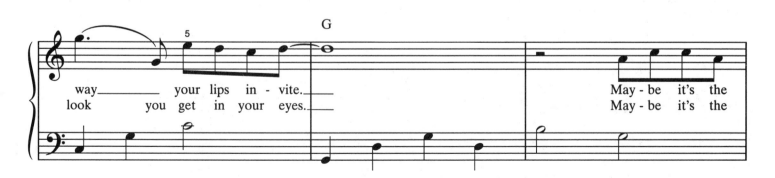

The Way - 5 - 1

WHITE FLAG

Written by
DIDO ARMSTRONG,
RICHARD NOWELS and ROLLO ARMSTRONG
Arranged by DAN COATES

White Flag - 4 - 1

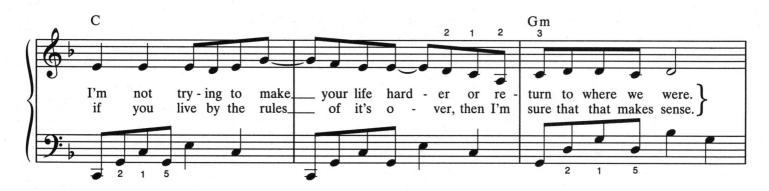

I'm not try-ing to make your life hard - er or re - turn to where we were.
if you live by the rules of it's o - ver, then I'm sure that that makes sense.

Chorus:

But I will go down with this ship, and I won't

put my hands up and sur - ren - der. There will be no white flag a - bove my

1.

door, I'm in love and al - ways will be.

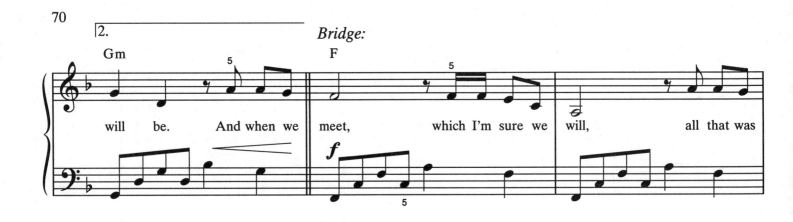

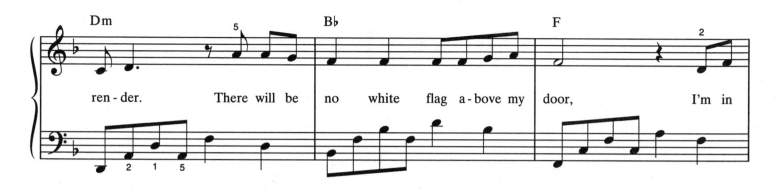

ren - der.　There will be　no white flag a - bove my　door,　I'm in

love　and al - ways　will　be.　I will go down with this

ship,　and I won't　put my hands up＿and sur - ren - der.　There will be

no white flag a - bove my　door,　I'm in love　and al - ways　will be.

YOU'RE STILL YOU

Words and Music by
LINDA THOMPSON and ENNIO MORRICONE
Arranged by DAN COATES

Slowly, with expression

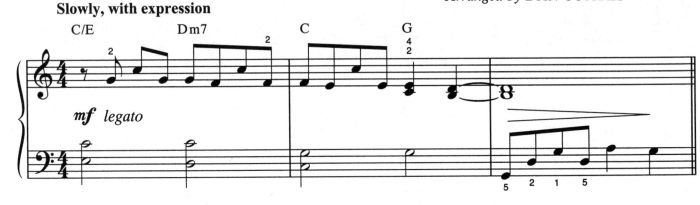

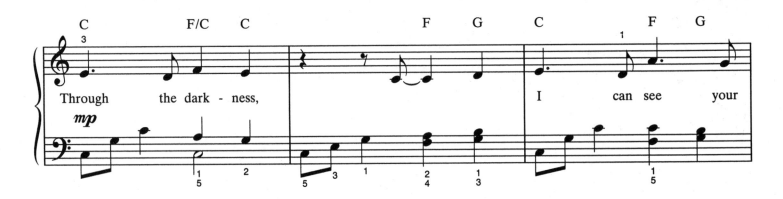

Through the dark - ness, I can see your light. And you will al - ways shine, and I can feel your

heart in mine. Your face I've mem - o - rized. I i - dol - ize just

You're Still You - 4 - 1

WHEN YOU TELL ME THAT YOU LOVE ME

Words and Music by
ALBERT HAMMOND and JOHN BETTIS
Arranged by DAN COATES

Verse 1:

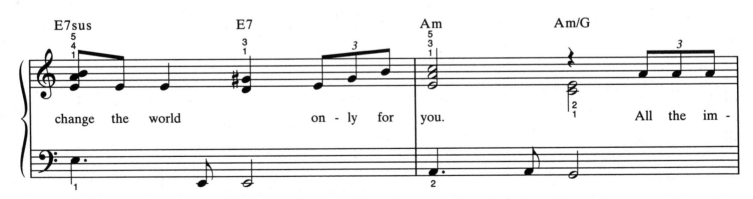

When You Tell Me That You Love Me - 5 - 1

80

shin - ing like a can - dle in the dark   when you tell me that you

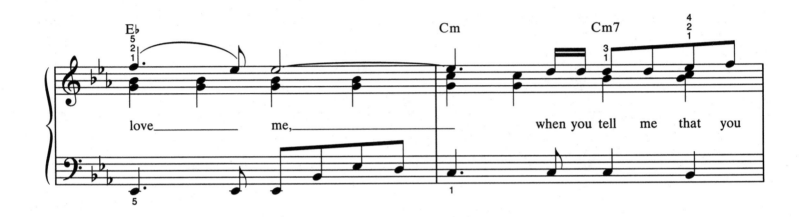

love _____ me, _____   when you tell me that you

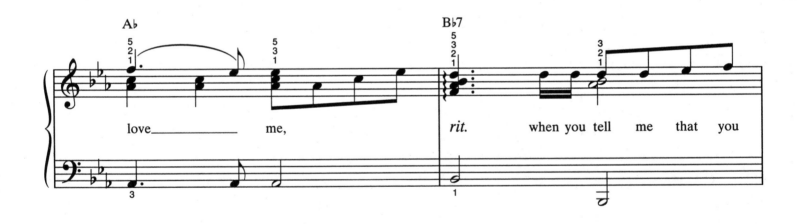

love _____ me,   *rit.*   when you tell me that you

love   me.

From THE POLAR EXPRESS

BELIEVE

Words and Music by
GLEN BALLARD and **ALAN SILVESTRI**
Arranged by DAN COATES

BECAUSE OF YOU

Words and Music by
KELLY CLARKSON, BEN MOODY
and DAVID HODGES
Arranged by DAN COATES

Slowly (♩ = 70)

(with pedal)

Verse:

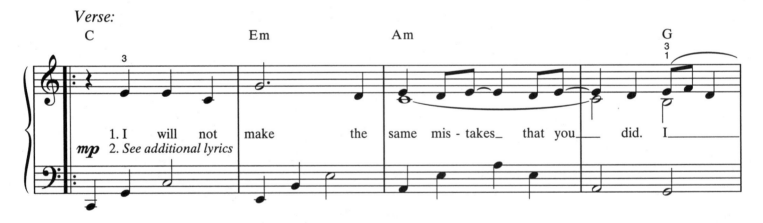

1. I will not make the same mis-takes_ that you_ did. I_
2. *See additional lyrics*

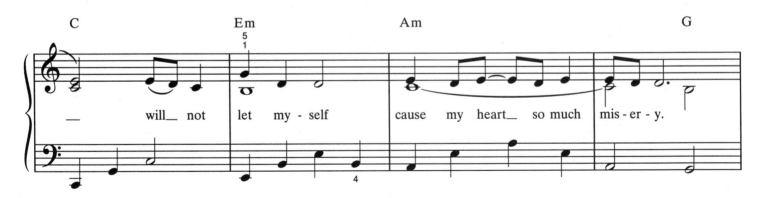

_ will_ not let my-self cause my heart_ so much mis-er-y.

Because of You - 5 - 1

Chorus:

Verse 2:
I lose my way,
And it's not too long before you point it out.
I cannot cry,
Because I know that's weakness in your eyes.
I'm forced to fake a smile,
A laugh every day of my life.
My heart can't possibly break
When it wasn't even whole to start with.
(To Chorus:)